DK READERS

Pre-level 1

Fishy Tales
Colorful Days
Garden Friends
Party Fun
In the Park
Farm Animals
Petting Zoo
Let's Make Music
Meet the Dinosaurs
Duck Pond Dip
My Dress-up Box
On the Move

Snakes Slither and Hiss
Family Vacation
Ponies and Horses
My Day
Monkeys
Big Trucks
John Deere: Busy Tractors
LEGO® DUPLO®: On the Farm
Star Wars: Blast Off!
Star Wars The Clone Wars: Don't
    Wake the Zillo Beast!
Cuentos de Peces en *español*
Días Llenos de Color en *español*

Level 1

A Day at Greenhill Farm
Truck Trouble
Tale of a Tadpole
Surprise Puppy!
Duckling Days
A Day at Seagull Beach
Whatever the Weather
Busy Buzzy Bee
Big Machines
Wild Baby Animals
A Bed for the Winter
Born to Be a Butterfly
Dinosaur's Day
Feeding Time
Diving Dolphin
Rockets and Spaceships
My Cat's Secret
First Day at Gymnastics
A Trip to the Zoo
I Can Swim!
A Trip to the Library
A Trip to the Doctor
A Trip to the Dentist
I Want to Be a Ballerina
Animal Hide and Seek

Submarines and Submersibles
Animals at Home
Let's Play Soccer
Homes Around the World
Bugs and Us
Train Travel
LEGO® DUPLO®: Around Town
LEGO® City: Trouble at the Bridge
LEGO® City: Secret at Dolphin Bay
LEGO® Pirates: Blackbeard's Treasure
Star Wars: What is a Wookiee?
Star Wars: Podracers, Go!
Star Wars: Luke Skywalker's
    Amazing Story
Star Wars: Tatooine Adventures
Star Wars The Clone Wars: Watch
    Out for Jabba the Hutt!
Star Wars The Clone Wars:
    Pirates... and Worse
Power Rangers: Jungle Fury: We Are
    the Power Rangers
Indiana Jones: Indy's Adventures
John Deere: Good Morning, Farm!
Gigantes de Hierro en *español*
Crías del Mundo Animal en *español*

A Note to Parents

DK READERS is a compelling program for beginning readers, designed in conjunction with leading literacy experts, including Dr. Linda Gambrell, Distinguished Professor of Education at Clemson University. Dr. Gambrell has served as President of the National Reading Conference, the College Reading Association, and the International Reading Association.

Beautiful illustrations and superb full-color photographs combine with engaging, easy-to-read stories to offer a fresh approach to each subject in the series. Each DK READER is guaranteed to capture a child's interest while developing his or her reading skills, general knowledge, and love of reading.

The five levels of DK READERS are aimed at different reading abilities, enabling you to choose the books that are exactly right for your child:

Pre-level 1: Learning to read
Level 1: Beginning to read
Level 2: Beginning to read alone
Level 3: Reading alone
Level 4: Proficient readers

The "normal" age at which a child begins to read can be anywhere from three to eight years old. Adult participation through the lower levels is very helpful for providing encouragement, discussing storylines, and sounding out unfamiliar words.

No matter which level you select, you can be sure that you are helping your child learn to read, then read to learn!

DK

LONDON, NEW YORK, MUNICH,
MELBOURNE, and DELHI

DK UK
Series Editor Deborah Lock
Senior Art Editor Tory Gordon-Harris
U.S. Editor Elizabeth Hester
Design Assistant Sadie Thomas
Production Claire Pearson
DTP Designer Almudena Díaz
Jacket Designer Peter Radcliffe

Reading Consultant
Linda Gambrell, Ph.D.

First American Edition, 2003
This edition, 2014
Published in the United States by DK Publishing
345 Hudson Street, New York, New York 10014

13 10 9 8 7 6 5 4 3 2 1
001—197250—January/2014

A catalog record for this book is available
from the Library of Congress.

ISBN 978-1-4654-1674-2 (Paperback)
ISBN 978-1-4654-1675-9 (Hardcover)

DK books are available at special discounts when
purchased in bulk for sales promotions, premiums,
fund-raising, or educational use.
For details, contact:
DK Publishing Special Markets
345 Hudson Street, New York, New York 10014
SpecialSales@dk.com

Printed and bound in China
by South China Printing Company

The publisher would like to thank the following for their
kind permission to reproduce their photographs:
(Key: a=above; c=centre; b=below; l=left; r=right t=top)

2 Tracy Morgan: (crb). **Ross Simms and the
Winchcombe Folk & Police Museum:** (cra). **Barrie
Watts:** (br). **4 Corbis:** Jeremy Horner (c). **6–7 Getty
Images:** Mike Timo. **7 Barrie Watts:** (br). **8 Tracy
Morgan:** (bl). **Corbis:** Bill Ross (cl). **8–9 Getty Images:**
Darrell Gulin. **9 Natural History Museum:** (bcr).
10–11 Getty Images: Jerry Driendl.
11 Stephen Oliver: (bc). **12 Stephen Oliver:** (bc), (br).
**13 Judith Miller & Dorling Kindersley & Bonhams,
Edinburgh:** (bl). **15 Getty Images:** Tom King (tr).
Stephen Oliver: (bc). **16–17 Gables Travels. 17 Guy
Ryecart:** (bc). **18–19 Stephen Oliver. 19 Stephen Oliver:**
(br). **Natural History Museum:** (bcl). **21 Corbis:** Craig
Tuttle (br). **22 Ross Simms and the Winchcombe Folk &
Police Museum:** (bl). **22–23 Jerry Young. 24–25 Jerry
Young. 25 Natural History Museum:** (br). **Jerry Young:**
(c). **26 Stephen Oliver:** (bl). **26–27 Getty Images:** Terry
Husebye. **27 Getty Images:** Paul Goff: (bl). **28 British
Museum:** (br). **32 British Museum:** (br).
Stephen Oliver: (c). Jerry Young: (bl)

All other images © Dorling Kindersley
For further information see: www.dkimages.com

Discover more at
www.dk.com

DK READERS

LEARNING
pre-level
1
TO READ

Colorful
Days

How many colors

green

yellow

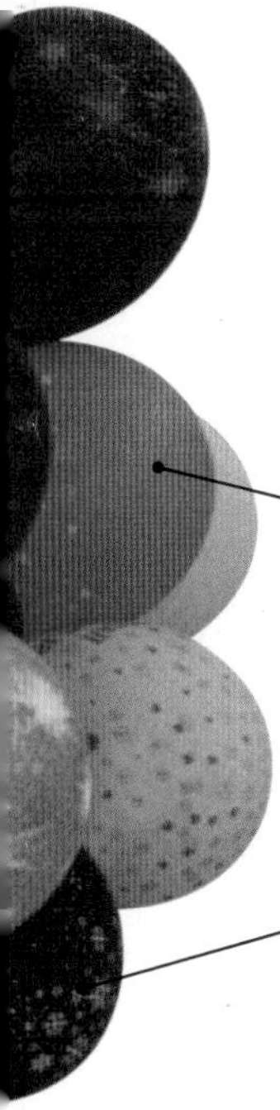

pink

red

Come and
play with me.

can you see?

eye

nose

mouth

white

We can play
in the cold,
white snow.

We can look at the purple flowers.

leaf

 purple

petal

blossom

We can run
around the trees
with the pink
blossoms.

 pink

petal

eye

gray

ear

fur

We can pet
the small,
gray rabbits.

We can sail
with the boats
on the blue water.

mast

sail

blue

deck

We can walk
through the
tall, yellow
sunflowers.

yellow

seeds

petal

orange

We can eat
a cold, orange
ice pop.

ice pop

stick————

boots

red

We can kick
the leaves and
pick the red apples.

tree

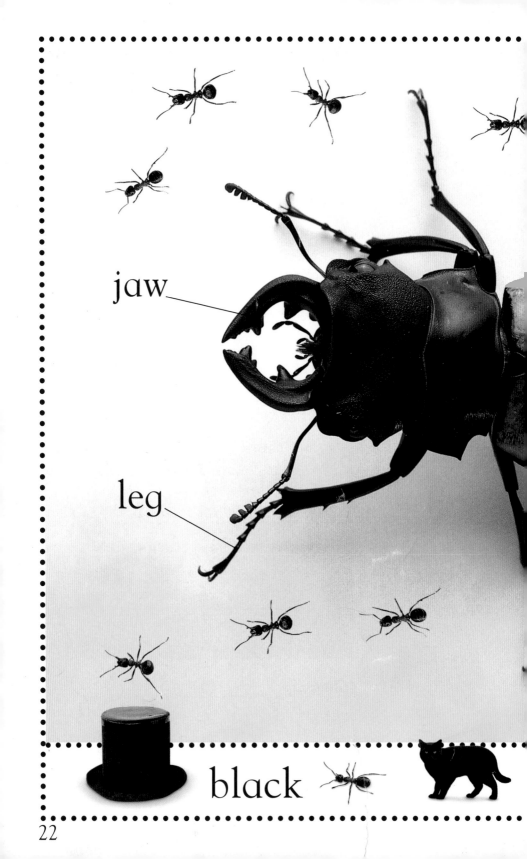

jaw

leg

black

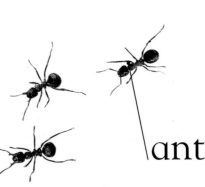

ant

We can crawl
like the ants and
the black beetle.

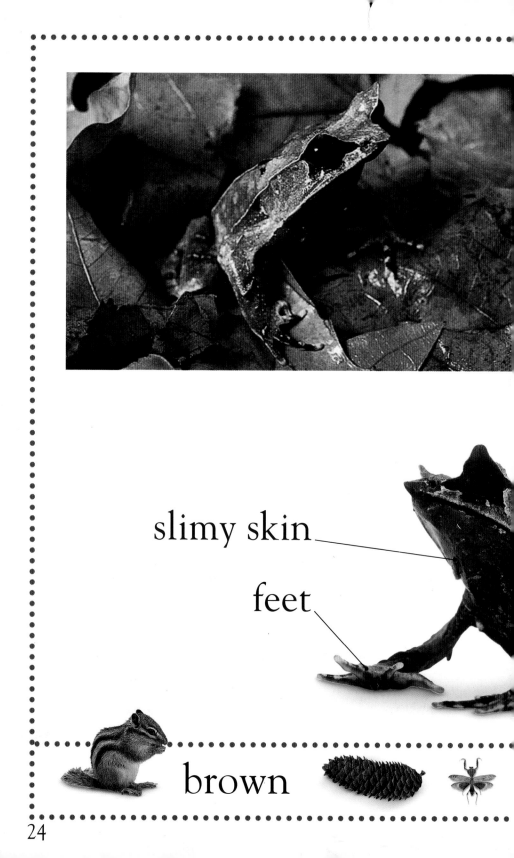

slimy skin

feet

brown

We can croak
like the small,
brown frogs.

branches

needles

green

We can run around
the tall, green trees.

We can hang
silver balls and
put on gold crowns.

silver

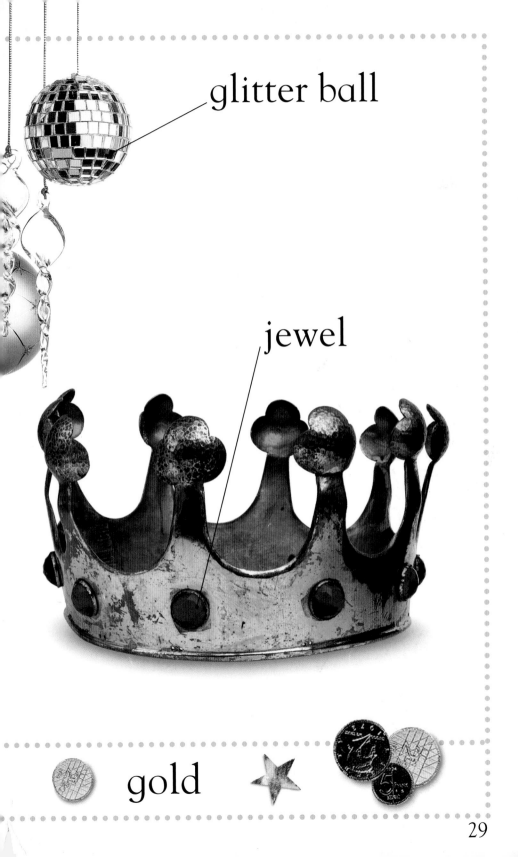

glitter ball

jewel

gold

How many colors

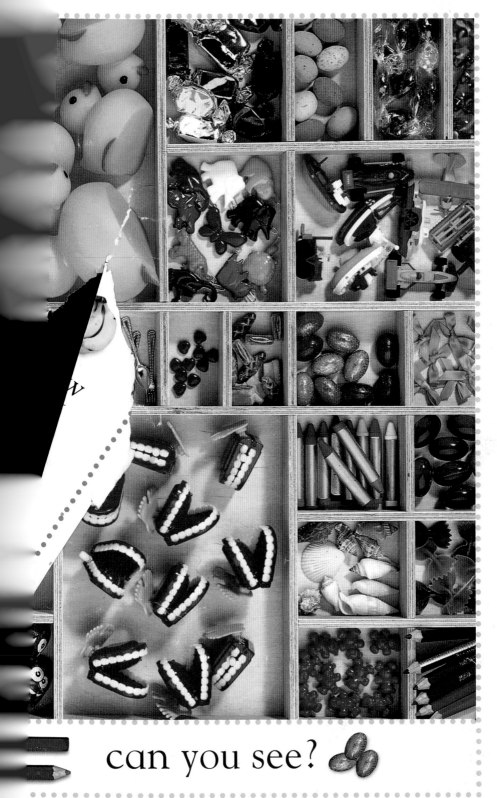

can you see?

Picture Word List

white
page 6

purple
page 8

pink
page 10

gray
page 12

blue
page 14

yellow
page 16

orange
page 18

red
page 20

black
page 22

brown
page 24

green
page 26

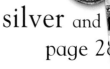

silver and
page 28

Index

DK READERS

My name is

_____

I have read this book

Date

_____